COLLINS AURA GARDEN HANDBOOKS

BONSAI

D1334037

ANNE SWINTON

COLLINS

Products mentioned in this book

Benlate* + 'Activex'	contains	benomyl
'Kerispray'	contains	pirimiphos-methyl
'Sybol'	contains	pirimiphos-methyl

Products marked thus 'Sybol' are trade marks of Imperial Chemical Industries plc
Benlate* is a registered trade mark of Du Pont's
Read the label before you buy: use pesticides safely.

Editor Maggie Daykin
Designers James Marks, Steve Wilson
Picture research Moira McIlroy

This edition first published 1988 by
William Collins Sons & Co Ltd
London · Glasgow · Sydney
Auckland · Toronto · Johannesburg

© Marshall Cavendish Limited 1985, 1988

British Library Cataloguing in Publication Data

Swinton, Anne
  Bonsai.——(Collins Aura garden handbooks).
  1. Bonsai
  I. Title
  635.9'772 SB433.5

ISBN 0–00–412379–4

Photoset by Bookworm Typesetting
Printed and bound in Hong Kong by Dai Nippon Printing
Company

Front cover: Acer palmatum
Back cover: Juniperus chinensis
Both by the Harry Smith Horticultural Photographic Collection/
Anne Swinton

CONTENTS

INTRODUCTION

The origins of bonsai are lost in the mists of time, but their cultivation probably began in China over 1,000 years ago as a result of the principles of Taoism. Followers of this religion believed that natural phenomena such as mountains, trees and rocks contained magic, and that miniature examples would possess it in concentrated form. Also, a contorted, gnarled shape was thought to represent the bodies of those in the world beyond mortality, where they would have attained great age. Out of these beliefs has developed a highly fascinating and rewarding form of horticulture – bonsai.

The earliest bonsai were the naturally dwarfed trees growing on mountains and were lifted when already old. Initially, these little trees were left in their natural shape but, in a country with such topographical variation, regional styles of bonsai developed during the Ming dynasty (1368-1644). Training was introduced to create 'flat top', 'pagoda' and other shaped specimens. But these training methods are now rarely practised in China, the Cantonese 'grow and clip' method having superceded them in the early 20th century.

In Japan, the history of bonsai covers a shorter timespan, the first authentic record being on a 1309 picture scroll by Takakane Takashina, known as the Kasugagogengenki. Other contemporary records indicate that during the Kamakura period (1180-1333), the aristocracy displayed bonsai in specially made ceramic pots that were placed on the verandahs of their homes.

During the 14th century, the increasingly powerful merchant classes became interested in the little trees, with the result that in order to satisfy demand, young trees were potted and trained using a method known as 'tako'. This involved coiling and tying the trees' trunks and branches with hemp string, to reduce the height and give a gnarled, twisted effect combined with an overall pyramidal shape.

From 1603-1867 Japan enjoyed a period of peace, during which the arts—including those associated with horticulture—were developed considerably. Landscape gardening reached new levels of excellence and scope for bonsai training was improved by the interest in the Southern school of painting, which was causal in the development of Literati style bonsai (see page 17). For a while during this period (Tokugawa, 1603-1867), rather grotesquely-shaped trees were considered good bonsai but, fortunately,

this fashion was a short-lived one.

Until about 1820, bonsai were potted into rather deeper containers than those used today, doubtless following the style of potting used by the Chinese. But by 1830, shallower pots in a wider range of styles were catalogued in *Kinsei-jufu*, published in that year.

The styles into which trees were trained were also changing, the tako-styled bonsai being no longer available. Naturally dwarfed trees from the mountains were highly prized (as now), and cascade, twin-trunk, weeping and other styles of younger bonsai were listed in nurserymen's catalogues of the period.

Certain species of tree were grown as bonsai in particular regions of Japan, such as Honai (Echigo province) where villagers still produce many thousands of 'Horai' syled *Pinus parviflora* (Japanese white pine) to satisfy demand. The shimofuri form is grafted on to *P. thunbergii* (Black Pine), trained by coiling the branches round pegs of mulberry wood, secured with rice straw and planted into fields for maximum growth. A sizeable bonsai is produced in about seven years by this method.

The fall of the feudal government in 1867 was followed by a major period of expansion in Japan. With the freedom to explore new ideas, and a broadening of horizons, a liberated society was quick to enjoy the beauty of bonsai, previously the exclusive property of the wealthy. More nurseries were set up to produce young but well-shaped trees and the skills involved in training them were further developed.

LEFT Trees without a branch misplaced – and water, used for its reflective qualities – blend perfectly in the Imperial palace gardens at Katsura, Kyoto.

RIGHT This *Juniperus rigida* grew for about 150 years on a mountain side, dwarfed by harsh conditions until collected, potted and further developed to its present beauty.

By the start of the 20th century the Japanese were exporting bonsai and the first exhibition of Japanese bonsai in London was held in 1909. There was considerable public interest and individual bonsai found their way into the country from time to time after that. However, it wasn't until the late 1950s that popular interest in the little trees began to grow.

For several years there was a popular misconception that these trees were of some special species that simply 'grew like that'. Bonsai were believed to be very difficult to grow and were surrounded by oriental mystique. Only within the last 10 to 15 years has an ever-widening group of enthusiasts been

Creating a successful bonsai involves patience, and a sense of artistry.
ABOVE Though appearing as a single tree in the raft style, these are, in fact, three young *Pinus thunbergii*, carefully presented.
RIGHT A 100-year-old *Cryptomeria japonica*, trained in formal upright style and only one-fiftieth of its natural size for that age.
ABOVE FAR RIGHT A young potentially well-shaped example of the Japanese white pine, *Pinus parviflora*, showing the purple flowers borne in May

sented, and over the years the same tree, cared for and continually trained, will develop the magnificence associated with a mature forest tree. And when several are arranged in the same container you can create a miniature forest.

The oriental mystique attached to bonsai is perhaps not totally misplaced, though misinterpreted. Bonsai training has developed far more in Japan than in China, largely due to the work of the Zen priests of the Tokugawa period. Zen is a uniquely Japanese form of Buddhism. It is a way of life, rather than a religion, in which great emphasis is placed on the importance of self-discipline, contemplation and preconceived ideas, and the tolerance and peace of mind to be gained by the practice of meditation.

The slow cultivation of bonsai and the patience therefore required to develop the trees was, for the priests, a form of meditation. There was no frustration in the knowledge that the tree would continue to grow and develop after their death, rather this helped them to appreciate the oneness of man with nature.

In teaching the art, the importance of the relationship between master and pupil was that during the long learning process respect for the master would transfer itself to the subject matter, thus producing a necessary reverence for the bonsai, along with an almost intuitive understanding.

This feeling sometimes develops in westerners who cultivate bonsai over a period of years. Starting with a love of trees and a willingness to try a new form of gardening results in the satisfaction of having been responsible for the raising of a miniature 'forest' which is at one and the same time a thing of beauty, timelessness and tranquillity.

able to start correcting these misconceptions among the general public. Now, very few people still compare bonsai training with foot binding in China, though too many still think that they are genetic dwarfs rather than normal trees. Changing also, is the mistaken belief that bonsai must be of great age to be worth having.

A bonsai is created by using a combination of fairly basic horticultural skills, artistry and perception. British trees can be trained as well as Japanese trees, and tropical varieties are not excluded. The range of styles is wide and the size may vary from 2-3 cm (1-1½in) to 1m (3ft 3in) or more. In the East, trees far larger than this are also trained, some as 'patio' trees in large tubs. There is much pleasure to be obtained from the charm of a 5-year-old bonsai, well shaped and pre-

SUITABLE SPECIES

Among the wide range of trees growing wild in Britain are many that are well suited to bonsai cultivation. The Oak (*Quercus*) and the Beech (*Fagus*) grow well from seed, their seedlings being naturally small-leaved are the best to select for training. Large-leaved trees such as the sycamore (*Acer pseudoplatanus*), plane tree (*Platanus × hispanica*) and Lime (*Tilia*) are best grown into bonsai over 30 cm (12in) tall, though Horse chestnut (*Aesculus*) leaves can be amazingly reduced.

Fagus sylvatica heterophylla. These five 10-year-old trees give an impression of far greater maturity. The finer, deeply cut leaf of this fern-leaf beech makes it particularly well suited to bonsai work and a good subject for 'forests'.

The English Elm (*Ulmus*), which can be obtained from suckers, and the Hornbeam (*Carpinus*), whose seeds have a two year germination period, make very finely-branched bonsai offering a very good sense of scale, especially in winter, as does the Hawthorn (*Crataegus*), with its tiny leaves and bonus of May flowers. Sadly, this last species – as with Oak (*Quercus*) and Crab apple (*Malus*) – is susceptible to mildew. Sufficient specimens of each should be obtained to allow you to discard any which show signs of disease.

Among the many flowering trees, the Crab apple is one of the finest and should be trained as a bonsai of 30cm (1ft) or more in height, in order that the blossoms and fruit are not disproportionate. Easily grown from seed which must be fresh, it will look well alongside Peach (*Prunus persica*), Apricot (*P. mume*) and Almond (*P. dulcis*). The wild Cherry (*P. avium*) offers the added bonus of fine autumn colour. To provide a season of blossoming bonsai one must also include the very early flowering winter Jasmine (*Jasminum nudiflorum*), grown from cuttings, and the Quinces (*Chaenomeles*), obtained from suckers.

Some trees look at their best in autumn, notably many members of the maple family (*Acer*) but also the Rowan (*Sorbus aucuparia*), Katsura tree (*Cercidiphyllum japonicum*) and Winged Spindle (*Euonymus alatus*), which also has an interesting bark.

The evergreens are an important group of trees, many of which make outstanding bonsai. Pines (*Pinus*) offer considerable variety in needle colour and bark texture and there is much variety also among the many

RIGHT *Acer palmatum* 'Chisio', here in its spring-time glory of cerise-red foliage, and with a recorded history of over 140 years.
BELOW A fine old *Crataegus monogyna*, ideal for many bonsai styles.

11

ABOVE *Juniperus chinensis* 'Sargentii' in a large pot, to encourage growth.

RIGHT *Pyracantha angustifolia* with bright red winter berries.

Juniperus, some of which have scale like leaves, others looking more like the foliage of the *Cryptomeria*. The Yew (*Taxus*), though poisonous, makes a good bonsai and has a striking golden form. A less common, though somewhat similar plant is the Western Hemlock (*Tsuga heterophylla*).

Some evergreens are classed as 'broadleaf', that is, their leaves are not adapted into scales or needles. The evergreen oak (*Q. ilex*) makes a fine bonsai, as does the *Pyracantha*, which additionally offers flowers and clusters of red or orange berries. Less usually seen as bonsai are Holly (*Ilex aquifolium*) though there are many good variegated forms available, Ivy (*Hedera helix*), for which the same is true, the rock rose *Cistus* and many others. However, it should be mentioned that the broadleaf evergreens are not well adapted to tolerate periods of cold, snow and frost and need some shelter from the worst of the winter weather.

For those who wish to grow bonsai for indoors there is a wide range of suitable warm climate and tropical trees. Choice can be made depending on the warmth of your house and factors such as availability of sunny windowsills or humid bathrooms; a conservatory can offer great scope.

Among the Citrus family the Grapefruit (*C. paradisi*) is probably the easiest to cultivate from pips, though none are too difficult and all are evergreen. The Pomegranate (*Punica granatum*) grows well from seed or cuttings and may be evergreen or deciduous depending on winter temperature. During a long hot summer the grower may be rewarded with a profusion of bright scarlet flowers but even without these the fine foilage makes this plant one of the finest indoor bonsai.

The Rubberplant (*Ficus*) family offer much scope. These may be grown from seed or small plants obtained from florists as houseplants and trained as bonsai. One of the best is the Weeping Fig (*F.*

A good woodland arrangement that is composed of 19 *Zelkova serrata*

benjamina) with its pendulous growth. It doesn't appreciate temperatures below 16°C (60°F) but the Moreton Bay Fig (*F. macrophylla)* with its bulbous trunk base and aerial roots is half hardy, as is the Ivy Ficus (*F. pumila)* which makes an excellent small bonsai.

For the adventurous, *Coffea arabica,* the commercial coffee plant, is an attractive candidate: fresh unroasted coffee beans must be obtained and high temperatures are required for germination. The red and yellow Guavas (*Psidium)* produce two different leaved plants and the West Indian Mahogany (*Swietenia mahogani)* becomes a pinnate-leaved tree with interesting bark.

Owners of rather cold houses could consider the Olive (*Olea).* There are several different types, some being available from herb plant specialists, others being grown from fresh olives. They all have a pleasant silver coloured foliage.

Palms, too, may be grown as bonsai. A box of dates will produce many *Phoenix dactylifera* which, with regular attention to their roots, will become miniaturised. *Cycads,* primitive plants that look like a cross between a palm and a fern, may also be grown from seed and trained in a similar way. They are worthwhile additions to an indoor bonsai collection, botanically most interesting yet, at the same time, easy to care for.

In a small book it is only possible to name but a few of the many tree species suitable for bonsai training. If you simply consider that in Japan the list would include Orchids, Dandelions, Primulas, Grasses, Bamboo and many other plants you will realise that the list of candidates is almost endless. All that is required is some knowledge of the natural habitat and growing conditions to succeed in growing healthy plants, in readiness for the all important training.

13

BONSAI STYLES

To the uninitiated, the idea of different styles in bonsai may seem unnecessary. After all, a tree is a tree. However, on closer examination it will be realised that these little trees take many shapes and forms, and for ease of reference these are described here and overleaf. All the styles except one can be found in nature with full-sized trees, the exception being the formal upright style which, nevertheless, looks incredibly 'real' in a well-trained specimen.

Formal Upright *(Chokkan).*
Very few are to be seen in Britain, perhaps because of the lack of much suitable starting material. This need not deter the enthusiast, who can grow *Pinus* or *Cryptomeria* species for the purpose. Chokkan trees have a straight vertical, tapering trunk from which the branches radiate in an even progression. The spacing between branches is greatest at the lower levels, branches becoming progressively both shorter in length and more closely spaced towards the top of the tree. Ideally, the branches are grown parallel to the soil, lower branches being thicker than upper branches.

Species trained in this style are usually evergreen, *Pinus thunbergii*, *Juniperus rigida* and *Cryptomeria japonica* being the most usual.

Informal upright *(Moyogi).* This style covers a wide range of types, from the natural-shaped tree as if grown in a field, to the curved trunked, more stylised pine shapes. There are probably more bonsai in this category than any other, it being suitable for all species of tree.

Twin trunk *(Sokan).* The most important aspect of Sokan trees is the relative thickness and length of the two trunks, which share a common base. Trees may also have three *(Sankan)* or five *(Gokan)* trunks and all three types may be trained in formal, informal, cascade, literati or other bonsai styles.

ABOVE *Chamae-cyparis obtusa*, in formal upright style.

RIGHT *Pinus parviflora*, being trained in 'Horai' style.

14

Slanting *(Shakan)*. Not an over-sized tree potted at an angle to reduce its height, a fault often seen, but a truly balanced bonsai that would look right growing over a stream or in any similar location.

Windswept *(Fukinagashi)*. Although superficially similar to a Shakan tree, the Fukinagashi is characterized by achieving balance despite the fact that all its branches grow from one side of the trunk or sweep in one direction. Such a bonsai could be imagined growing on a windy hillside or near the coast.

Multiple trunk *(Kabudachi)*. Rarely seen, these bonsai have numerous trunks arising from a single root. Elm *(Ulmus)*, Yew *(Taxus)* and Quince *(Chaenomeles)* are among the species that some-times grow in this manner. To be really successful, there must be a good relationship between the thickness and lengths of the individual trunks, as in twin trunk *(Sokan)* trees. The usual shape is that of the informal upright *(Moyogi)* bonsai.

Raft *(Ikada)*. Such a bonsai is created from a tree that is initially faulty, having all its branches growing from one side of the trunk. When potted lying down, with the branches going upwards towards the sky, these become trunks of trees, joined by the original trunk. Roots begin to grow from the first trunk and eventually the old rootball can be cut off, leaving a most attractive 'group' of trees which are, in fact, one. Any species of tree can be trained in this manner, although it is more usually confined to conifers – especially *Pinus parviflora* – the Japanese white pine. The deciduous Larch *(Larix decidua)* is very suit-able and roots faster than pines.

ABOVE *Ulmus parvifolia*, in sloping trunk style. Rough bark and tiny leaves are special features of this species.
RIGHT twin-trunked *Cryptomeria japonica*.

LEFT This *Juniperus rigida*, like most literati styled bonsai, is evergreen.
BELOW *Acer buergeranum* showing the training roots and crown.
FAR BELOW Broom-style *Zelkova serrata* is enhanced by the shallow, oval container.

Broom (*Hokidachi*). A well-named style, the bonsai being shaped like an old-fashioned birch broom. There are two main types, the first having a length of trunk topped with branches all radiating from a single point and the second, similar in silhouette but with the branches tapering evenly upwards on the upper two-thirds of the trunk. A particular feature of Hokidachi bonsai is the profusion of fine, twiggy growth, without knots or lumps to mar the taper of the branches. Almost all examples of this style are of the Japanese Elm (*Zelkova serrata*) which grows readily from seed or cuttings, though the shrub *Spiraea* offers the same potential for fine, twiggy growth.

Cascade (*Kengai*). In this bonsai the trunk or trunks appear to fall over the side of the pot, which must be deep to give visual balance. As the trunk may descend considerably more than the depth of the pot, these bonsai are normally displayed on tall stands. Few are seen in Britain, their everyday storage presenting some problems, but most species can be trained in this way. In Japan, most of the Kengai bonsai tend to be evergreen.

Semi-cascade (*Han kengai*). These elegant bonsai have their trunks descending below the rim of the pot, though not below the base of the pot which is between a normal and cascade pot in depth. This style is seen more often than the Cascade and there is a very wide range of suitable varieties.

Literati (*Bunjingi*). These strange bonsai have a slim, wandering trunk crowned with a small area of branches, the whole being potted into a very small, usually round pot. The style evolved from the cultural movement Nanga, followed by the artists of the Southern School of Chinese landscape painting. The bonsai display the artists' search for freedom of expression though the Western mind more often likens them to the brush strokes of oriental caligraphy. In fact, this very clearly shows the difference in interpretation of the Eastern and Western mind; to the Easterner caligraphy is a demonstration of considerable discipline, exactly opposite to the freedom of the literati bonsai.

Group planting (*Yose-ue*). Groups of trees planted together in a shallow tray to give a woodland effect are comparatively modern and becoming increasingly popular. No doubt this is due to the fact that very young trees in a group quickly give the effect usually obtained only with a much larger, more mature single tree. Generally the group is confined to a single species though, if successful, a mixed group can be striking. Designs for these plantings are being constantly developed and improved upon.

Rock grown (*Ishitsuki*). There are two forms of rock grown tree, in the first of which a tree or trees will actually be planted into a rock. The hole for planting may be man-made or natural and the finished effect has a landscape-like quality. Though any tree will successfully grow this way, it is more usual to plant conifers in rocks.

The second form of rock planting is to train the roots of a bonsai to grow over a piece of rock and into the soil below (in a pot). This is time consuming, both in the initial work and in the subsequent period while the roots develop and the crown of the tree is trained, but the end result is very dramatic and well worth the trouble. Because of the suitability of their roots for this treatment, almost every example seen is of the species *Acer buergeranum*, the Japanese Trident Maple, and as these maples have small leaves and magnificent autumn colour they are worth obtaining. They can be readily grown from seeds or cuttings.

The Japanese categorize many other styles of bonsai, such as 'weeping branch' (which is a growth form rather than a style) or 'drift wood', seen on old pines and junipers where much of the trunk and branches are of bleached dead wood, but the most important shapes have been described above. In the following pages the methods used to obtain these shapes will be shown.

CULTIVATING A BONSAI COLLECTION

There are several ways of obtaining the starting material for a bonsai collection, the cheapest and most popular being from seeds. These may be purchased from garden centres or nurseries, or collected from woods, gardens, even from streets, when the seeds fall from the trees in abundance in autumn.

In nature, the seeds of hardy trees lie on the forest floor all winter, covered by a thin layer of leaves which keep them moist, until they germinate in spring when the temperature rises sufficiently after a long, dormant period of cold. When planting such seeds in a seedtray, therefore, it should be remembered that a period of cold must precede the warmth required for the seeds to grow.

A seed tray is prepared by putting a layer of drainage material, such as gravel, at the bottom followed by a layer of sieved soil mixture. Most trees grow well in a mixture of good potting compost (not soilless), leaf-mould and sand, using equal parts by volume. When the seed tray has been filled with this mixture it should be gently firmed down. Seeds may be sprinkled or spread in rows on this surface and then covered with only their own depth of the soil mixture or sand. The prepared tray should then be watered by either standing it in a container of water or by using a watering can with a very fine rose and allowing any surplus water to drain away.

The seed tray is then netted to protect its contents from cats or mice and stood outside in a cold part of the garden. It is important to check it from time to time to ensure that it does not dry out during the winter. In March or April the seed tray may be placed in a greenhouse to accelerate germination, but the minute seedlings begin to appear the tray should again be placed outside in a moderately sunny location and watered regularly. If seeds are sown in early springtime rather than autumn, the seedtray should be

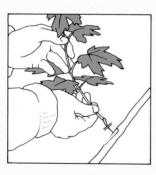

1. Remove a healthy young side shoot from branch, with a heel of older wood attached.

2. After trimming the heel, insert the cutting into the rooting medium, then firm.

3. Once rooted, cuttings should be potted up individually, ready for training as bonsai.

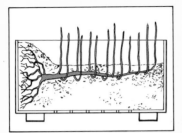

FAR LEFT Tree planted on its side for training in Raft style. **LEFT** Once the trunk produces roots, original rootball is removed and trunk and 'branches' potted for further training.

placed in a refrigerator for six weeks to give the seeds the cold they require.

Flat-dwellers or others who wish to grow their bonsai indoors need not despair at this point. Tropical varieties of tree are suitable for indoor cultivation and many seeds can be obtained from the fruit in any greengrocers. The seeds are placed in a seed tray in the same manner as for hardy seeds but the tray should then be placed in a position where they receive a bottom temperature of 21°C (70°F). It is a wise precaution to water the seed tray with a mixture of Cheshunt compound (from any good garden shop), to prevent the risk of damping off of the emerging seedlings (a condition in which seedlings rot at the point where stem meets soil).

Once the seedlings germinate they need a sunny location in which to grow into sturdy, short-jointed seedling trees.

Seedling trees. Impatient collectors can short-cut the growing process for British tree varieties at least, by collecting seedling trees from the wild. This is a simple process, rather akin to transplanting seedlings from a seedtray into a pot. You must have permission from the landowner to dig up wild trees, but once this is obtained all you will require is a trowel. Dig seedlings,

preferably of interesting shapes or compact growth, during the winter months when the weather is comparatively mild. Take care to disturb the root-system as little as possible and plant in a suitable sized flower pot with plenty of drainage material in the base. Water and place in a sheltered position out of doors. Once growth starts in spring, the tree is ready for the initial pruning that will eventually turn it into a bonsai.

Cuttings are a suitable means of obtaining some varieties, though trees such as Oak (*Quercus*), Beech (*Fagus*) and Silver Birch (*Betula*), cannot be grown this way. Other species however: *Cotoneaster, Pyracantha* and, in warm climates, Pomegranate (*Punica*) are readily grown.

Softwood cuttings are taken from non-flowering shoots of the current year's growth, in June. To prepare a tray or pot for the cuttings, fill it with a mixture of peat and sharp grit (equal quantities by volume). Vermiculite or polystyrene granules can be substituted for the grit, having the advantage of being clean and lightweight. Prepare the 10cm (4 in) long cuttings by removing the leaves on the bottom third of the cutting, dipping the stem in 'Keriroot' hormone rooting powder and inserting it up to about a third of its length

19

1. Set hardwood cuttings in a V-shaped trench, with 2.5cm (1in) of sand in the bottom to prevent rot at base of cutting.

2. Check that the cuttings are at correct sloping angle (not upright), with the cut end resting on sand base.

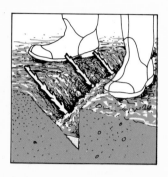

3. Carefully push the soil back into trench, firming down well with your foot to prevent frost lifting cuttings.

into a hole made in the mixture by using a pencil or similar tool.

The tray should then be carefully watered and placed on a bottom source of heat at about 16°C (60°F), wrapped in a tent of polythene to keep a high humidity around the cuttings. Cuttings may be sprayed lightly if they appear to be drying out a little, but take care not to make the mixture soggy. Once rooted (new growth will appear), the cuttings should be transplanted into pots, disturbing their roots as little as possible. Plenty of light will be required for these cuttings to root well and subsequently grow.

Semi-hardwood cuttings For people with a cold frame, these cuttings of suitable trees may be taken between July and September. A rooting mixture similar to that described above is used, but the cuttings will be larger, about 15cm (6in) and are taken with a 'heel' of old wood attached. Remove any very young growth, trim the heel and remove some lower leaves, then insert the cutting into the rooting medium. Then water the cuttings and place them in a closed cold frame. They will need to be sprayed daily to maintain the correct humidity and the frame should be covered with sackcloth during sunny periods to help maintain a stable temperature.

In spring the cuttings which have rooted can be potted up. Those which have formed callouses are generally discarded although, if they are of a rare variety, the callous may be pared off and the cutting reinserted. This method of propogation is used for such species as *Juniperus*.

Hardwood cuttings, for those with a garden, are very easy to deal with. Prepare a V-shaped trench in a well drained, sheltered, fertile part of the garden and place 2.5cm (1in) of sand along the bottom. Take ripe cuttings (with no soft, green wood), about 15-38cm (6-15in) long, and lay them against the sloping side of the trench with the bottom in the sand. The soil should then be pushed back into the trench and firmed in so there is no risk of movement to the cuttings caused by frost action or wind. These cuttings should be left for a year to 18 months before being lifted and potted up in the spring.

TRAINING BONSAI

Once you have several healthy young trees growing in pots it is time to think about the training needed to control and develop the shape of the future bonsai. Novices are usually rather nervous about pruning, thinking that they will hurt the trees, whereas in fact, it is an essential part of the process of keeping bonsai healthy, vigorous and bushy.

To prune a tree properly it is important to understand its natural growth habit. Among the deciduous trees there are some that produce new shoots and leaves throughout the growing season. This group includes Maple, Hawthorn, Hornbeam, Elm, Cotoneaster, Larch, Redwood, and Swamp Cypress, also the evergreen Japanese Cedar, the tender Citrus and Pomegranate. When the leaves of these trees open in spring, shoots are produced both from the tips of the branches and from the buds on the side of the branches. To maintain size shoots should be removed when they elongate, leaving only a leaf or two at the base.

Generally one is encouraging a bushier, twiggy growth, in which case shoots should only be partly removed. If encouraging growth in a certain direction, however, a shoot should be pruned to just above a leaf which points in the direction that future growth is desired. A subsequent shoot will grow from the dormant bud at the base of the leaf in the required direction. Much of this

Unwanted branches – those too low or directly opposite well-positioned branches – should be removed (thick lines). Finer growth should be trimmed (dotted lines) to encourage further branching.

FAR LEFT Anchor one thick and one thin wire as described in main text then, side by side, wind them round and up the trunk, keeping spacing even, to point A. Then continue with thin wire only.

LEFT Slender branches need only one wire. Anchor round trunk as indicated.

type of pruning, which is carried on throughout the growing season, is done with finger and thumb, though scissors may be used. Unhealthy trees should not be pruned like this. In fact, it is unlikely that the growth they could produce would demand pruning.

A second group of trees have two main periods of growth during a season. Among deciduous trees the most noteable examples are the Beech, and the Oak. Of the conifers, the most frequently seen bonsai with this habit is the Juniper. It is important to work on such trees when they are growing, in spring, and again in mid to late summer.

Beech trees produce from each dormant bud a shoot which lengthens, carrying about five leaves. This shoot must be shortened to the required number of leaves while it is still very young and soft. If this process is delayed, even for a week or two, the next crop of buds will have begun to form at the tips of the shoots and pruning will remove them. Punctual pruning ensures that new buds develop where you want them to, keeping the tree compact. The same process is repeated in late summer.

Evergreens of the juniper type also must be promptly pruned. The highly modified scale leaves will elongate considerably if allowed, resulting in a scraggy, untidy tree, but if such shoots are pinched back as they appear, the foliage will remain in the nice compact shapes for which these trees are so well known.

Young growth on *Juniperus, Cryptomeria, Chamaecyparis* and similar evergreens should always be removed by pinching out with finger and thumb. Using scissors would leave unsightly brown marks.

In winter, trees such as the Horse Chestnut, Ash and Oak carry a dominant bud at the tip of each shoot which, if allowed to grow in spring, produces a long, thick shoot of rather ugly appearance. Although this can be removed by subsequent pruning, it is a better policy to examine trees of this type in December and gently remove such buds. Smaller, dormant buds further back along the shoots will have time to develop before spring and the bonsai will produce numerous small, fine shoots instead of one large one.

Pruning pines. This is rather different to any other species, pines having only one main period of growth in a year. In spring, the pine produces a 'candle' from which the new season's needles then grow.

Once the 'candle' has extended, but before the needles appear, it should be broken or cut off at its base. This results in the tree producing three or four new buds around the cut candle; these develop during the early summer. Branches of vigorous pines such as the Scots pine (*P. sylvestris*) or the Japanese black pine (*P. thunbergii*), may be pruned with scissors or secateurs during mid summer, promoting the development of hidden dormant buds which will become side branches of the bonsai in subsequent years.

Sometimes, an otherwise nice bonsai will have one ugly thick branch that needs to be removed. Depending on size, secateurs, bonsai pruners or even a small saw can be used but major work of this type should only be carried out in winter when the tree is dormant, and even then, *not* during spells of frost or other extreme conditions. All major pruning cuts must be treated with a pruning compound without delay, to prevent the entry of disease-producing organisms.

Wiring. The shapes of bonsai may also be induced or modified by wiring, a process by which wire, traditionally copper, but nowadays often plastic-coated garden wire, is wound round a branch or trunk which is then bent into the desired position. The wire, if of the correct thickness, will hold the branch in the new shape until, weeks, months, or even years later, depending on the species and the age and thickness of the branch, it will stay that way and the wire can be removed.

Among deciduous and broadleaf evergreen trees this wiring is normally only carried out on young growth which is still green. Wood shoots are liable to break if bent and have the habit of unbending themselves when unwired, even if left for a considerable time. The conifers are not a problem in this respect. Given strong enough material, even a 50-year-old trunk can be persuaded to bend and ultimately remain in the new position. Some species, noteably *Prunus* and *Cryptomeria*, are sensitive to the feel of wire on their bark. Plastic-coated wire should always be used for such trees.

As a general rule, deciduous trees are wired during the summer and the conifers in winter or spring. Many trees become very brittle for a short period in spring when the sap is rising, so this particular time must be avoided.

When wire is applied to a branch, one end must first be anchored by winding it twice around the trunk. It should then be wound around the branch, not so tightly that it cuts in, nor so loosely that there are gaps between wire and branch. Coils should be evenly spaced and the wire should travel the length of the branch. Usually, this means starting with a piece about twice as long as the branch to be wired.

Once wiring is complete the branch should be carefully bent into the desired position – it must not be bent backwards and forwards as this can easily kill a branch. If the new shape does not please you, the branch should be unwired and left for six months before you rewire it into a new position. Where a trunk is being wired, two wires, one thick and one thin, are used - see illustration top left – and both wires can be anchored by pushing them into the soil around the base of the trunk.

Once a tree is wired it should be examined carefully at least once a month to ensure that the wire is not cutting into and marking the bark. Should this begin to happen before a branch has set, the wire should be removed without delay and new wire applied. There is no excuse for wiremarks, it is clearly neglect.

POTTING

To understand bonsai potting you first need to know a little about how tree roots grow and behave in open ground. A tree growing in a field has two sorts of roots. One or several tap roots grow vertically downwards, to obtain water and act as anchors. Other, more finely divided roots radiate outwards from the tree, as feeding roots, their tips absorbing from the soil the minerals, salts and other requirements of the tree. As the crown of the tree increases in size, so these roots spread, drawing nutrients from fresh areas.

When a bonsai is growing in a pot, the crown is regularly trimmed to keep it a desired size. The roots however continue to grow and over a period of one to three years, depending on the species and age of the tree, they will become potbound. Any plant in this situation begins to require a great deal of water, puts up little new growth and if left longer, begins to die.

The solution for the average pot plant is to transplant it into a bigger pot. With a bonsai however, the tree is being pruned to a certain size so a bigger pot would look wrong and would provide for a larger rootball

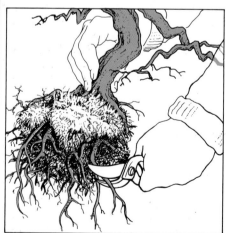

To keep growth in check, straggly roots should be removed, then the rootball reduced by a quarter of its size.

than tree, an unnatural balance. For these reasons, root pruning is carried out instead. This shortens the feeding roots, which divide more, becoming more efficient as they have more tips to absorb nutrients. The tap roots are not required so they are also removed. They cannot fulfil their function as anchors and water is given to the tree as required (see page 31). The pruning process is normally carried out in spring before leaf opening.

Early autumn is another time when conifers may be repotted, and this should be carried out when the bonsai in question is getting a little short of water (but not bone dry). Lift it out of its pot and wrap the rootball in a damp cloth while you prepare the pot. This should be washed and the drainage holes covered with plastic mesh, then a layer of fine pebbles is spread over the bottom of the pot for drainage. On top of this, place a thin layer of the potting mixture and on this a thin layer of finer (sieved) potting mixture.

Now prepare the bonsai for potting. An examination of the rootball will show a number of large roots winding around. These should be carefully eased away from the main mass of roots and allowed to hang. The outer part of the finer root area should then be treated in the same way. A chopstick or knitting needle

FAR LEFT Bonsai with trimmed rootball, carefully repositioned in a ready-prepared pot.
LEFT Dry soil is added and eased between the roots with the aid of a chopstick. Then gently firm down.

is an ideal tool for the job. Next, trim back the roots, using a clean, sharp pair of scissors and leaving 65-75 per cent of the rootball intact. This will leave some of the cut fine roots sticking out from the rootball, which is now ready to be repotted.

Placement of the bonsai is of importance to achieve the best possible effect. The tree should be nearer to the back of the pot than to the front, and to left or right of centre unless the pot is round or hexagonal – in which case the tree should be in the middle. When soil is added it should slope upwards from just below the rim of the pot to the base of the bonsai trunk, giving a natural effect and allowing the display of roots radiating from the trunk. Many bonsai are potted too high or too low in the pot, so this is a point that you need to watch.

When adding fresh potting compost (which must be sieved), it is far easier if the compost is bone dry. This enables it to trickle between the roots of the bonsai (aided by the use of a chopstick), and hold the bonsai in position. Once this is completed, gently firm the soil and water the bonsai thoroughly, allow it to drain and place it in a sheltered position for a few weeks. Newly-potted trees should be watered only when they are getting dry, at which time they should be watered thoroughly. Constantly soggy conditions are likely to cause rotting of the cut roots and in consequence, the possible death of the tree.

Potting mixtures. These sometimes worry the novice but, for most trees, a mixture of good garden loam, well-rotted leafmould and coarse, clean sand or grit will make a very suitable compost. The contents should be sterilised before use, and if leafmould is collected from woodlands this can be simply achieved by baking in the oven in a biscuit tin with a well-fitting lid. Some trees dislike lime. These must be provided with a lime-free compost and peat substituted for leafmould. Conifers, as a group, prefer a very sandy soil so add a higher proportion of sand to their mixture. The items mentioned can be varied in proportion to suit any particular tree.

Group plantings. Once the potting technique for one tree has been mastered, you might like to consider the possibility of a group planting. In this, the positioning of the numerous trees is all-important; the potting techniques for each tree remains the same.

To start, select 6-12 young trees of the same species but varying heights. Taller trees should have thicker trunks; discard any that do not. Divide the remainder into three groups: those that are upright and fairly regular in branch growth, those with a tendency to lean or branch to the left and those that lean or have a tendency to branch to the right.

Groups are always planted with an uneven number of trees, so, if you have an even number, one tree must be discarded. All the trees in the group will be planted in the rear half of the pot, so first position the upright, regular trees, with the tallest nearest the front. If there are fewer than seven trees, one large tree should be chosen as a focal point and the others grouped in relation to it.

If you have more than seven, there can be two focal points: one each to right and left of centre. The trees leaning or growing to the left can be arranged behind and around the left side of the pot, the others on the right side.

As perspective is important, it is generally best to have the biggest trees in front of the others so that they appear nearer than they are.

Once the positions have been decided, pot the bonsai as described on page 24. Remember as you do so that the final contours of the soil are important to the finished effect. It is most usual to have the highest level of soil just to the rear of the largest tree and to gradually slope it down towards the smaller trees at the outer side and rear edges of the pot.

Root-clasping rock bonsai. This type of bonsai is a great challenge to anyone's potting talents. As the initial work takes a year or two, an *Acer buergeranum* should be obtained and potted into a deep container to encourage long roots to grow. In a year or two there will be a sufficient number of these for the real work to be carried out.

First select a suitable rock. It must be very hard, dark in colour, and large enough to allow for future growth of the bonsai and its roots.

The current season's growth on *Pinus parviflora* should be wired in the autumn, after the summer needles drop. This allows light in between the branches, encouraging more budding and branching. If this is not done, lower branches gradually die back through lack of light.

Wash all the soil off the roots of the bonsai, taking care not to damage the long roots. Then decide the position of bonsai and roots over the rock. The bonsai should now be put aside, the roots protected from drying out with a wet cloth, while the rock is prepared for the planting. The roots will need to be firmly attached to the rock and this is effected by attaching to the rock a thin wire, by means of a strong adhesive such as epoxy resin, or by inserting wires with a collar of lead into little crevices in the rock's surface, using a centre punch.

Once there are plenty of secure wires, the areas of the rock to be covered by roots should be liberally smeared with a mixture of clay, peat and water. This is a very sticky process, but helps to secure the roots and gives them nutrients.

The rock is now ready for the bonsai, which should be carefully positioned. Gently press the roots into the clay and secure them with the wires, leaving the trailing wire ends hanging at the base of the rock.

Now liberally coat the rock and roots with more of the clay mixture before covering them with a layer of moss.

At this stage you should have, in effect, a bonsai sitting on a moss-covered lump with a fringe of long roots hanging from its base. String must be tied around the rock in several directions; garden string is preferable as it will rot in a year or two. The root over rock bonsai should now be potted into a deep container so that the soil level reaches about one-third of the way up the rock. One year later, in early spring, the bonsai should be repotted so that the soil covers only enough of the rock base to secure it in the pot. Gradually, the moss can be removed. Everyday watering should help.

Once the roots are exposed check them to ensure that they fit closely to the rock. If there are gaps, apply more moss and tie the string tighter. Once the roots are exposed to the air they will begin to grow bark and become inflexible. They will also thicken at a slower rate so, for the best effect, they should remain covered for a few years.

A similar, though simpler method is used to plant bonsai in a rock (using either a hollow rock or a piece of tufa – which can be chiselled out as required – instead of a pot). The hollow in which the tree is to be planted should be coated with a mixture of clay, peat and water, as previously described. This helps to secure the bonsai, which is then potted in the hollow.

Once potting is complete, a thin layer of the mixture is applied over the surface of the soil and moss is attached to prevent the usually rather small amount of soil from being washed away when you water the bonsai. This is particularly relevant if the tree has been planted in the side of the rock.

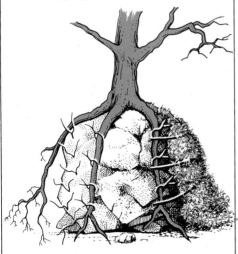

The bonsai is first positioned on the prepared rock and the roots anchored with wires. Once secured, cover roots.

PRESENTATION

Any bonsai can be likened to a good picture. That is to say, if it is to give maximum enjoyment, it should not only be appropriately 'framed', but also 'hung' in the best possible position for viewing.

Select bonsai pots not only for their size, but also for their shape, colour and compatibility of styling with the features of the particular bonsai. All pots must, of course, provide good drainage and be frost proof for all hardy bonsai.

In general terms, the size of the container is dictated by the bonsai, the depth equalling the trunk diameter, length being about two-thirds the height of the bonsai and width two-thirds of that. The colour range is generally confined to dark brown, sand, red/brown, silver grey or green/grey, unglazed, these subtle tones suiting nearly all bonsai. Some glazed pots are available, but these are mainly used to harmonise with the blossoms of flowering trees. Whatever pot is used, it must not be glazed inside or underneath, because it must be porous.

All bonsai pots have feet, some being sturdy and rectangular (ideal for an old pine), others of a more ornate, scroll type design known as 'cloud foot', which is very light and elegant.

The majority of pots are rectangular or oval. They may have lips turned inwards or outwards, straight or sloping sides, or feature an impressed pattern. Literati bonsai are usually potted into very small round, square or hexagonal pots and cascade trees into deeper versions of these shapes.

Bonsai pots are not easy to obtain, being almost exclusively available only from the very few specialist bonsai nurserymen. As they will last a lifetime, it is a good idea to obtain a stock of them for use when needed, adding to your collection whenever the opportunity arises to do so.

LEFT Antique, glazed and unglazed bonsai pots.
ABOVE RIGHT A fine *Punica granatum*, 'The Pomegranate', seen here with the clear yellow autumn foliage, before it falls.
RIGHT 'Mame' bonsai in autumn colour (from right) *Parthenocissus* 'Veitchii'; *Ulmus procera*; *Spiraea japonica*; *Cotoneaster horizontalis*; *Pyracantha* hybrid.

When a pot has been selected and a tree potted into it, judicious use of moss or fine gravel on the soil surface considerably improves the overall effect by giving the bonsai a very 'natural' setting.

A bonsai is best viewed from near eye level, so those hardy trees which live in the garden should be placed on staging in a sheltered area where there is good light. Staging can be built to match the surrroundings: for example, tree trunks and rough hewn planking in a rustic garden, building blocks and paving slabs for a town patio, or stone pillars and cut stone slabs for a period garden. Indoor bonsai are best placed on gravel in a very shallow tray and positioned in an uncluttered area with good light. Bamboo matting is also very handy and attractive and can be used whenever you want to display a hardy bonsai indoors for an evening or two. With both indoor and outdoor bonsai, trees that are being trained are best kept separate from those already in display pots.

GENERAL CARE

A bonsai is capable of living through many generations of a family, so its daily care is of more than passing importance. As this care varies from season to season, I have covered it in this way – beginning with winter.

As with all living plants a bonsai will not survive without water. The frequency of watering depends on many factors, the chief of which are the state of growth of the plant and the weather.

In winter, hardy bonsai living outside will need very little over and above what falls as rain. Indoor trees will need to be checked, as moisture in the soil will be lost by evaporation, even though the bonsai will be doing little, if any, growing.

Spring is a dangerous time. As leaves and shoots begin to grow, the water requirement of the bonsai increases enormously and this usually coincides with a change in the weather from wet and cold to breezy and dry. Bonsai should be watered whenever they have used most (not all) the water in the pot.

RIGHT An outstanding example of *Pinus parviflora* in the raft style, displayed in the bonsai garden of Mr. Murata, its creator, in Omiya, Japan. To maintain this standard requires regular handwork and an ideal climate, with a long summer and a short winter.

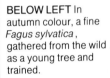

BELOW LEFT In autumn colour, a fine *Fagus sylvatica*, gathered from the wild as a young tree and trained.

By summer, the weather should, with luck, be very warm, perhaps with a breeze and strong sunlight. Under these conditions bonsai will require watering thoroughly once a day, preferably in the early morning or late evening and in exceptional weather possibly both. Indoor bonsai also will have increased their water requirement and therefore should be checked every day.

In autumn trees begin the chemical changes which cause leaf drop and dormancy. Their water needs drop and they must not be over-watered at this time as, with lower temperatures, especially at night, rot could be caused in the roots.

Such watering attentions through the seasons will keep a bonsai alive but, for maximum health, bonsai should be fertilized. A general purpose liquid fertilizer suits most trees and as a general rule should be applied regularly for 2 months once leaves have opened and again in late summer for a month. Coniferous trees can be fertilized three or four weeks earlier than deciduous trees. Flowering trees should not be fertilized once flowers are fully open and for at least a month after that, while fruits begin to set.

Hardy bonsai should be given especial consideration during the summer holiday period. The neighbour who waters the garden is unlikely to realize the amount of water that a bonsai in a pot will drink on a hot sunny day, with possibly disastrous results. The easiest solution is also the best. Prepare in good time by giving your neighbour a few young bonsai as a present in the early spring. You then each care properly for the other's trees when on holiday.

If such a convenient neighbour is not to hand and you have a garden with a spare flower bed in a shady part, the trees can be partially buried, leaving the crowns and branches uncovered. The whole area should be thoroughly soaked before your departure, running a hose on it for 24 hours if possible. Provided the area is shady and really well soaked,

Acer palmatum offers good colour in spring, when its newly opened leaves are tinged with rich brown. After a few weeks this clears to green. Many *Acer palmatum* – as is the case with this well-trained 40-year-old example – also have outstanding autumn tints.

the bonsai should last for two weeks.

If this method is not possible, the trees should be taken into the bathroom and the curtain closed to keep out the sun. A number of old bath towels or, better still, ICI Capillary Matting, should be placed on the bottom of the bath and saturated and the well watered bonsai stood on this. With a little practice beforehand, it may be possible to leave the cold tap dripping to keep the matting moist. If this *is* done it is essential to ensure that the bathplug cannot fall into the hole, otherwise a flood might result.

All deciduous bonsai that have to be left like this in hot weather can, with advantage, have much of their foliage removed. This cuts down the loss of needed water from the tree.

In winter, hardy bonsai may need some protection from severe cold. They do not appreciate temperatures dropping below freezing for any length of time because the continued cold causes the whole rootball to freeze and this results in badly damaged roots. In cold parts, trees can be buried in the ground in a sheltered spot; in such circumstances they almost look after themselves. Alternatively, use can be made of sheds, garages, greenhouses or similar outhouses, remembering that the bonsai can get no rain and will need watering once or twice a week. Snow is not a problem to bonsai; in fact, it protects them from icy winds and frost.

PESTS AND DISEASES

Another form of care for bonsai is the protection of the tree against pests and diseases. Fortunately, most bonsai being well cared for and healthy there are few problems of this sort, but simple curative measures should be taken if any of the following become troublesome.

Ants. These are sometimes seen running up and down the trunk of a bonsai and their presence usually means there is another pest, such as aphid on the tree. Once these are removed, the ants are easily dealt with by immersing the tree totally in a bucket of water to which a spoonful of washing-up liquid has been added. Leave 30 minutes then drain. If the ants had formed a nest in the rootball, they and it will be drowned.

Aphids. These well-known pests tend to accumulate at leaf and shoot growing time on maples. Acer bonsai are sensitive to commercial sprays so the treatment described above for ants should be used to effect a cure.

Crown Gall. Bacteria-filled galls formed on the damaged roots of plants, this disease is aggravated by waterlogging. Fortunately, it is rarely seen on bonsai but, if spotted, all affected roots must be removed and drainage improved.

Damping off. A condition affecting seedlings which rot where their stem meets the soil level. Watering seed trays with Cheshunt, according to the manufacturer's instructions, helps prevent this problem.

Mealy bugs. These look like pale woodlice, only smaller, and appear on indoor plants, including cacti and bonsai, looking like little pieces of cotton wool. If ignored, they will multiply rapidly. On a small bonsai, remove them by hand.

Mildew. This fungal disease appears as a white powder on leaf surfaces in summer. If seen on very young, untrained trees, these are best discarded. Otherwise, Benlate + 'Activex' may be used.

Red spider mite. This is a serious pest of both indoor and outdoor species, sucking sap and causing rapid deterioration and death of affected bonsai. Affected trees should be sprayed with 'Sybol' or an insecticide containing dimethoate, repeated a fortnight later. In hardy bonsai, conifers are mainly affected during very hot, dry periods. Raising the humidity around the trees seems to help prevent this trouble.

Scale insects. These limpet-like insects infest both indoor and out-door varieties, being seen attached to bark of trunk or branches and the underside of leaves. On a bonsai these pests can be removed by hand (cotton wool buds dipped in methylated spirits is a simple way) and the tree sprayed with an insecticide such as 'Kerispray', 'Sybol' or one containing dimethoate.

Woolly aphid. These aphids protect themselves with a cottonwool-like coating. They are most usually seen on pines, and may be controlled by applying forceful sprays of 'Sybol' solution.

SIXTY OF THE BEST

A bonsai is a miniature version of a mature tree growing in the wild and, to be completely successful, it should give the illusion of scale. All of the trees and shrubs recommended on the following pages have that potential.

Acer buergeranum

Japanese trident maple. Hardy deciduous. Suited to many styles including groups, but especially root-clasping rock bonsai. A vigorous grower featuring spring and autumn colour. It can be grown from seeds, cuttings or layers.

Repotting Every two to three years, in spring.

Pruning Summer or winter.

Pests Greenfly in late spring.

Acer palmatum

Japanese mountain maple. Hardy deciduous. Suited to many bonsai styles and renowned for its autumn colour. There are also many *A. palmatum* cultivars which are suitable as bonsai. The species grows from seed, cultivars must be propogated from cuttings or grafted plants.

Repotting Every one or two years, in spring.

Pruning Summer or winter.

Pests Greenfly in late spring.

Acer pseudoplatanus

Sycamore. Hardy deciduous. Rather large-leaved bonsai grown from seed or wild plants.

Repotting Every one or two years, in spring.

Pruning Summer or winter plus bud prune in winter. Defoliate totally in June to reduce leaf size.

Aesculus hippocastanum

Horse cheshnut. Hardy deciduous. Easily grown from 'conkers'. Large leaves reduce well.

Repotting Every one or two years, in spring.

Pruning As for *Acer pseudoplatanus.*

Azaleas

Evergreen half hardy. Trained for their beauty in flower, small flowered types should be grown, usually from cuttings.

Repotting Annually in spring. Azaleas are lime haters so use lime-free loam, leafmould peat and sand in equal quantities by volume.

Pruning Twiggy growth immediately following flowering, large branches in winter.

Special needs This species must not be allowed to go dry at any time. Winter protection advisable.

Betula pendula

Silver birch. Hardy deciduous. Suited to most bonsai styles and features attractive silvery bark when mature, together with a fine clear yellow autumn colour. Easily grown from seed or wild seedlings.

Repotting Every two years.

Pruning Prune young shoots to three buds during growing season. Total defoliating in late June encourages branching.

Special needs Appreciates cool, partially shaded position during the summer months.

Acer buergeranum

Buxus sempervirens

Box. Hardy evergreen. Being very small leaved it is ideally suited to training as small bonsai in upright styles and has little green flowers in late spring. This is most usually grown from cuttings.

Aesculus hippocastanum

Acer palmatum 'Seigen'

Repotting Every two years.
Pruning Pinch back new growth in late spring and late summer. Do not wire this species.

Carpinus betulus

Common hornbeam. Hardy deciduous. Suited to many styles and worth growing for its fine twiggy growth and attractive bark. Will also flower and fruit under bonsai training. The Japanese form *C. laxiflora* also has excellent autumn colour. Growth is by slow germinating seeds.
Repotting Every two years, in early spring.
Pruning Young growth during growing season, branches in summer or winter.
Pests Can be troubled with aphids, leaf cutter bees or mildew.

Cedrus libani

Cedar of Lebanon. Hardy conifer. Well suited to groups or individual upright styles and grown from seed.
Repotting Every two years, in spring or autumn, adding extra sand and leafmould to the mixture.
Pruning Young shoots whilst green; older wood in autumn

Azalea

Cercidiphyllum japonicum

Katsura tree. Hardy deciduous. Offers a host of features, early spring flowering, spring leaf colour, fine red bark and autumn colour rivalling the Maples. In addition, it is easily trained in upright styles and grown from seed or cuttings.

Repotting Every one or two years, in early spring.

Pruning Continue with trimming throughout late spring and summer; branch prune in summer or winter.

Special needs Leaves are easily damaged by wind or shortage of water in summer.

Chaenomeles japonica

Japanese quince. Hardy deciduous. All the quinces are popular as bonsai because of their long flowering period in early spring. They are easily grown from suckers or cuttings.

Repotting Every year, in spring or autumn.

Pruning Remove long shoots, retain short (flowering) shoots.

Special needs Fertilize with high phosphate fertilizer in late summer.

Chamaecyparis obtusa

Hinoki cypress. Hardy evergreen conifer. This slow-growing tree is rarely seen in England, most supposed Hinoki cypress being grafted plants of *C.o.nana gracilis*, which are not suitable to train as their growth rate is negligible. Hinoki cypress can be propogated by seed or cuttings and trained into various styles.

Repotting Every three years, in early spring, using extra sand and leafmould.

Pruning Pinch out new growth in late spring and late summer, branches in summer or winter.

Pests Red spider mite can be a problem during hot dry spells.

Citrus

Tender evergreen. Any of the citrus family are suited to indoor cultivation as bonsai, appreciating a sunny location and growing from seed at a temperature of 18.5°C (65°F).

Repotting Every two years, in late spring, using lime-free mixture.

Pruning During the growing season.

Pests Susceptible to scale insect, mealy bug and red spider.

Cotoneaster horizontalis

Hardy deciduous. Flowering and fruiting, together with very early spring growth and fine autumn colour, the variety can be used in many bonsai styles. Grows well from seeds, cuttings or wild seedlings.

Repotting Every two years, in early spring.

Pruning Trim throughout the growing season. Only wire young green growth.

Pests Occasionally crown gall on imported plants.

Crassula sarcocaulis

Half hardy evergreen. This makes a fine small bonsai for indoor cultiva-

Chamaecyparis

tion in winter. It carries many pink flowers (there is also a white form) in late summer which have a very unpleasant smell.

Repotting Every two years, adding plenty of extra sand to the mix.

Pruning As required during the summer, except for six weeks before flowering. Do not wire this plant.

Special needs Keep on the dry side in winter.

Cryptomeria japonica

Japanese cedar. Hardy conifer. This lovely evergreen turns a bronze colour in the autumn and winter and makes good formal upright or group bonsai. Grown from seed or cuttings.

Repotting Mid to late spring, with extra sand and leafmould.

Pruning Constantly pinch out new growth during the growing season; branches may be removed in summer or winter.

Daphne retusa

Hardy evergreen. The dark-green leaves and scented pink flowers in late spring make this a worthwhile bonsai subject. Grows from seeds or cuttings.

Repotting Every two years, in spring.

Pruning Immediately following flowering.

Elaeagnus umbellata

Hardy deciduous. Attractive coloured foliage plus flowers in late spring and red fruits in the autumn, this is suited to informal styles. Grown from seed.

Repotting Every two years, in spring.

Pruning After flowering.

Euonymus alatus

Winged spindle. Hardy deciduous. A very desirable plant for bonsai training, with flowers and berries, a most interesting 'winged' bark and very fine autumn colour. Can be grown from seed or cuttings.

Repotting Every two or three years in spring, using a little extra loam in the mixture.

Pruning Late winter, early spring.

Special care Dislikes very cold spells or dry summers.

Cotoneaster horizontalis

Euonymus alatus (before pruning)

Fagus svlvatica

Beech. Well suited to bonsai training, with pleasing autumn colour and holding dead leaves in winter. *F.s.purpurea*, the copper beech, and *F. crenata*, the Japanese white beech, are also recommended.

Repotting Every one or two years, in spring.

Pruning Trim back shoots immediately after growth in late spring and late summer.

Pests Whitefly in summer.

Ficus benjamina

Weeping fig. Tender evergreen. This well known houseplant makes a good bonsai in a centrally heated house with a light position.

Repotting Every one or two years, in late spring.

Pruning Pinch back young shoots as they develop.

Pests Scale insect, mealy bug and red spider mite.

Ficus macrophylla

Moreton bay fig. Tender evergreen. An unusual tree, growing a bulbous base to its trunk and producing aerial roots. It can be grown from seed and requires only modest heat.

Repotting/pruning As for *F. benjamina*

Forsythia

Hardy deciduous. Easily grown from cuttings; noted for its bright yellow spring flowers.

Repotting Every year or two, after flowering.

Pruning Immediately after it has flowered.

Fraxinus excelsior

Common ash. Hardy deciduous. A pinnate-leaved tree which offers most in winter with its silver bark and black buds, it is readily grown from either seed or wild seedlings.

Repotting Every two years, in early spring.

Pruning Remove dominant buds in midwinter; prune shoots during the growing season and branches in summer or winter.

Fuchsia magellanica 'Pumila'

Hardy deciduous. A small flowering fuchsia which trains into an excellent small bonsai, it should be protected from cold and wet in winter. Can be grown from cuttings, and alpine nurseries are sources of stock plants.

Repotting Annually, in spring.

Pruning Prune hard at repotting time; subsequently shoot-nip until early summer.

Special care This bonsai should be fertilized weekly throughout the growing season.

Ginkgo biloba

Maidenhair tree. Hardy deciduous conifer. A primitive tree, usually trained to resemble a candle-flame shape, it gives magnificent autumn colour of primrose yellow. Is grown from seed or cuttings, but the latter are more likely to be successful, if you're a novice.

Repotting Every year, in spring, with plenty of sand and leafmould in the mixture.

Pruning Immediately following growth, in late spring and late summer.

Special care If large branches are removed, cut ends must be protected against rot.

Hedera helix

Common ivy. Hardy evergreen. An unusual but very good candidate for bonsai training. Many coloured-leaved cultivars are also suitable to grow from cuttings.

Repotting Annually, in the late spring.

Pruning Shoot-prune during the growing season. Summer defoliating encourages branching, smaller leaves and richer colours on variegated forms.
Pests Scale insect.

Jasminum nudiflorum
Winter jasmine. Hardy deciduous. Grown for the beauty of the clear yellow flowers in very early spring. Propogated from cuttings.
Repotting Every one or two years, immediately after flowering.
Pruning After flowering.

Juniperus chinensis

Juniperus chinensis
Chinese juniper. Hardy conifer. A classical species for bonsai and suited to training in all bonsai styles. It is grown from cuttings.
Repotting Every two or three years, in spring or autumn, with extra sand and leafmould.
Pruning Pinch back young shoots as they grow in late spring or late summer. Branch-prune in winter or summer.
Pests Red spider mite.
Special note: *J. Communis* and *J. rigida* are among the many other junipers suited to bonsai training.

Laburnum anagyroides

Golden rain tree. Hardy deciduous. Grown for the racemes of golden flowers, these trees should be trained as bonsai of at least 30cm (12in) in height, to allow for the flowers.

Repotting Every year, in spring

Pruning After flowering, can be prone to die back.

Larix decidua

European larch. Hardy deciduous conifer. This graceful tree makes a beautiful and elegant upright or group bonsai. Even young bonsai produce cones which persist on the branches for four years. They grow well from seed.

Repotting Every two years, in early spring, adding extra leafmould and sand.

Pruning Pinch back young shoots as they grow; branches may be pruned in summer or winter.

Malus baccata

Crab apple. Hardy deciduous. Grown for the spring blossom and fruits which are cherry-sized. They are easy to train and grow readily from fresh seed.

Repotting In early spring.

Pruning Trim after flowering; shorten long branches in summer.

Pests Sometimes affected by aphids and mildew. Tolerant to sprays.

Metasequoia glyptostroboides

Dawn redwood. Hardy deciduous conifer. A graceful and unusual bonsai with good autumn colour from its feathery foliage and attractively coloured and textured bark. Grow from cuttings.

Repotting Every two years, in spring, with extra leafmould and sand in the mixture.

Pruning Nip back young shoots as they grow; branch-prune in summer or winter.

Special care. A little winter protection is recommended.

Morus nigra

Black mulberry. Hardy deciduous. Makes an interesting informal upright bonsai, the leaves reducing well in size.

Repotting Every two years, in early spring.

Pruning Pinch back young shoots as they grow; do not prune large branches.

Parthenocissus quinquefolia

Virginia creeper. Hardy deciduous. A suprisingly successful bonsai with the bonus of fine autumn colour.

Repotting Every two years, in early spring.

Pruning Prune climbing shoots back to no more than three leaves, in early summer.

Larix decidua

42

Picea

Spruce. Hardy conifer. Several varieties of the attractive species are suitable for training in upright or group styles of bonsai. Some can be grown from cuttings, others from seed.

Repotting Every four to six years, adding extra sand and plenty of leafmould.

Pruning Pinch back new growth as it appears.

Pests Some *Picea* may attract red spider mite.

Pinus

Hardy conifer. Responds well to bonsai training in all styles and grows well from seed. There is surprising diversity of colour and form in the many varieties available.

Repotting Every four or five years, in spring or autumn, with a very open mixture. Older trees should have a high proportion of leafmould and sand in the mixture.

Pruning Break off 'candles' in spring, prune branches of vigorous varieties in summer; wire new growth in autumn.

Pests Woolly aphid.

Platanus × hispanica

London plane. Hardy deciduous. Suited to informal upright styles, the large leaves reduce well in size and older trees display the mottled, peeling bark that is such a feature for the species. They grow well from seed.

Repotting Every two or three years, in early spring.

Pruning Pinch back young shoots as they develop.

Malus 'The Big Crab'

Parthenocissus 'Veitchii'

Podocarpus macrophyllus

Half-hardy conifer. A little known tree with attractive yew-like foliage. It must have winter protection and grows from cuttings.

Repotting Every three or four years, in late spring or the early autumn.

Pruning Avoid winter months.

Populus alba

White poplar. Hardy deciduous. This and other poplars make interesting informal upright or group bonsai.

Repotting Every year, in spring.

Pruning Trim young shoots in summer.

Special care Keep well watered in summer.

Prunus avium

Gean. Hardy deciduous. This cherry is grown for its flowers in May, with fruit and autumn colour as an extra. Fresh seeds germinate quite well.

Repotting Every year, in autumn.

Pruning After flowering; do not branch-prune in winter.

Special note Other *Prunus* also make excellent flowering bonsai.

Punica granatum

Pomegranate. Tender deciduous/evergreen (dependant on winter temperature). Probably the best choice for indoor bonsai in a wide range of styles. It grows readily from seeds or cuttings; flowers are a special bonus during an especially fine summer.

Repotting Every two years, in late spring or early summer.

Pruning During the summer months.

Pests Scale insect.

Pyracantha angustifolia

Firethorn. Hardy evergreen. Grown for the clusters of white flowers in early summer and red or orange berries in the autumn. It responds well to training. Grows from seeds or cuttings.

Repotting Every two years, in spring.

Pruning After flowering. Any wiring must be carried out on young, green shoots.

Pyracantha angustifolia

Quercus hybrid

44

Quercus

Oak. Hardy. Mostly deciduous, but one or two evergreens. Oaks grow well as informal upright or group planting bonsai. Acorns should be planted while fresh. Early growth is quite rapid.

Repotting Every two years, in spring.

Pruning Remove dominant tip buds in winter; trim back young shoots in summer.

Pests Oak galls and mildew.

Salix babylonica

Weeping willow. Hardy deciduous. An attractive tree, rapidly grown from cuttings and trained by bending the branches in the hands. An advantage is that it can spend the summer standing in water.

Repotting Twice a year, in spring and late summer.

Pruning Remove young shoots from the underside of branches as they appear.

Pests Caterpillars during the summer.

Sophora japonica

Sequoia sempervirens

Redwood. Though the largest of trees in its native California, the redwood can be trained as a bonsai of the smallest size. It grows well from seed, which keeps for years.

Repotting Every two years, in spring, using sandy compost.

Pruning Pinch back young shoots during the growing season.

Special care Protect from extremes of cold in winter. Enjoys high humidity in summer.

Sophora japonica

Japanese pagoda tree. Hardy deciduous. A pretty, pinnate-leaved bonsai once it begins to branch. It grows from seed.

Repotting Every two years, in spring.

Pruning Remove growing tip and defoliate in early summer to encourage branching growth.

Pests Scale insect.

Sorbus aucuparia

Mountain ash/rowan. Hardy deciduous. A very pretty tree which makes a most attractive small- or medium-sized bonsai with finely serrated, pinnate leaves and fine autumn colour. Grows from seed or wild seedlings.

Repotting Every two years in spring.

Pruning Nip back young shoots as they grow; wire in summer if this is necessary.

Spiraea japonica

Hardy deciduous. This pretty flowering shrub makes an outstanding small bonsai. Grows readily from seed or cuttings.

Repotting Every two years, in spring.

Pruning Trim in late spring and again after flowering. Remove completely any long straight shoots.

45

Syringa vulgaris
Lilac. Hardy deciduous. A well-known plant which trains easily and grows from cuttings or suckers.
Repotting Every two years, in spring.
Pruning Trim shoots as required in summer.

Tamarix pentandra
Tamarisk. Hardy deciduous. Usually trained like the willow, as a weeping tree, it bears feathery pink flowers in late summer.

Repotting Every two years, in mid spring.
Pruning During the winter.

Taxodium distichum
Swamp cypress. Hardy deciduous conifer. Justifiably becoming more popular as a bonsai now its many virtues are better known. Suitable for all upright styles and the fine feathery foliage offers autumn colour. Grows well from cuttings.
Repotting Every two years, in spring or early autumn.

Taxodium distichum

46

Pruning Nip back the new shoots in summer.
Special care This bonsai tolerates standing in water during the growing season.

Taxus baccata
Yew. Hardy conifer. The churchyard tree makes a good evergreen bonsai. Can be grown from cuttings or from wild seedlings.
Repotting Every two years, in spring.
Pruning Trim young shoots in late spring and late summer.
Pests Scale insects.
Special note This tree is very poisonous in all its parts. Keep away from young children and from all animals.

Tilia cordata
Small-leaved lime. Hardy deciduous. Makes a surprisingly good bonsai in informal styles. Grows well from seed.
Repotting Every two years, in early spring.
Pruning Trim shoots during the summer.

Trachycarpus fortunei
Chusan palm. Half hardy evergreen. An unusual and successful subject for bonsai training.
Repotting Every year, in late spring.
Pruning None required.
Pests Scale insects.

Tsuga heterophylla
Western hemlock. Hardy conifer. An ideal tree for small or large spreading upright styles of bonsai. Grows from seed or cuttings.
Repotting Every three years, in spring.
Pruning Pinch back young shoots as they appear, prune older wood in autumn.

Ulmus parvifolia
Chinese elm. Hardy deciduous. A very beautiful fine-leaved, rough-barked tree, suited to most styles of bonsai. It can be grown very well from cuttings.
Repotting Every two years, in spring or early autumn.
Pruning Trim new shoots as they appear throughout the summer.
Pests Is susceptible to Dutch elm disease.

Ulmus procera
English elm. Definitely worth having in view of the great losses in standard trees. It can be cultivated from suckers and makes an attractive informal bonsai.
Repotting Every two years in spring.
Pruning During the summer months.
Special note Spraying with systemic insecticide during springtime helps remove the likelihood of Dutch elm disease.

Wisteria floribunda
Hardy deciduous. Trained to flatter the long racemes of flowers which hang in profusion in late spring. Can be grown from seeds, cuttings, layers, or grafts.
Repotting Every year, in early spring.
Pruning Prune hard in early spring; trim in summer.
Pests Scale insects.

Zelkova serrata
Hardy deciduous. Related to the elm, these trees have earned their position as one of the finer species for bonsai cultivation. Has lovely autumnal colouring.
Repotting Every two years, in spring.
Pruning Any time.
Pests Scale insects and aphids.

INDEX AND ACKNOWLEDGEMENTS

Picture credits

Anne Swinton: 6, 31

All other pictures Harry Smith Horticultural Photographic Collection/Anne Swinton

Artwork by Richard Prideaux and Steve Sandilands